The Immune System

The KidHaven Science Library

The Immune System

by Gloria Boudreau

KIDHAVEN
PRESS™

THOMSON
——✳——™
GALE

San Diego • Detroit • New York • San Francisco • Cleveland
New Haven, Conn. • Waterville, Maine • London • Munich

© 2004 by KidHaven Press. KidHaven Press is an imprint of The Gale Group, Inc.,
a division of Thomson Learning, Inc.

KidHaven™ and Thomson Learning™ are trademarks used herein under license.

For more information, contact
KidHaven Press
27500 Drake Rd.
Farmington Hills, MI 48331-3535
Or you can visit our Internet site at http://www.gale.com

LIBRARY OF CONGRESS CATALOGING-IN-PUBLICATION DATA

Boudreau, Gloria
    The immune system : by Gloria Boudreau.
      v. cm. — (KidHaven science library)
    Includes bibliographical references and index.
    Contents: The immune system fights disease—Specialists at work—
Problems of the immune system—Man-made immunity.
      ISBN 0-7377-2077-8 (hbk. : alk. paper)
      1. Immune system—Juvenile literature. [1. Immune system.]
     1. Title. II. Series
      QR181.8.B685 2004
      616.07'9—dc22

                          2003018300

Printed in the United States of America

Contents

Chapter 1

The Immune System Fights Disease

In the late 1880s, Russian scientist Elie Metchnikoff was examining wandering cells in sponges and starfish. He looked through his microscope and watched them move. They would stick out one part of their cell body and pull the rest after it— push, pull, push, pull. They would surround bits of food and eat them. Metchnikoff thought about what he was seeing. Perhaps these cells ate live germs, too. Then his thoughts took another leap. Maybe this is what happens with the cells in blood. Perhaps this was how the body fought off disease.

Although Metchnikoff had not seen the cells eat germs, he believed in his theory. His theories later proved true. He had began the search to understand the body's defenses. Future scientists discovered more about blood cells and their effect on disease germs. They discovered other germ-fighting blood cells. Now doctors refer to all of these body defenses as the immune system. They use their knowledge to prevent and cure disease.

 The Immune System

The immune system is the body's built-in protection against injuries and disease. Without an immune system, people could not recover from illness. Cuts and burns would not heal. In healthy people, though, the immune system is on twenty-four-hour alert. Its cells and chemicals are ready to attack invaders and repair damaged areas of the body. Blood quickly transports these healing elements to places where they are needed.

Lifesaving Blood

Most of the ingredients in blood are not part of the immune system. Still, they are important helpers.

Russian scientist Elie Metchnikoff believed that cells in human blood were responsible for fighting disease.

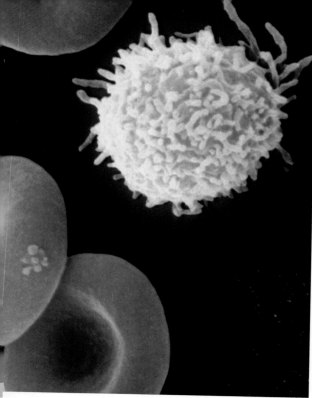

One such helper is a watery fluid called **plasma**. More than half the blood is plasma. Substances the immune-system cells use to stay alive, such as nutrients from food, are dissolved in plasma. In addition, plasma contains many individual cells. The body makes these blood cells in the center—**bone marrow**—of certain bones. When cells leave the bone marrow, they enter the plasma and travel throughout the body.

Helper red blood cells (left) support the immune system's white blood cells (pictured).

Helper red cells make up 45 percent of blood. They carry a gas people breathe in and that cells need—**oxygen**. Immune-system cells combine this oxygen and the food in plasma to make energy they need to fight disease.

Other helpers are cells that break into pieces before they leave the marrow. These tiny bits are called **platelets**. Platelets cause blood to become thick, or clot. Clotting allows an injury to be sealed up until the immune system completes its work.

Plasma, red cells, and platelets all support the white blood cells of the immune system. In a healthy adult, one teaspoon of blood contains 20 million to 50 million white cells. That number will increase during an infection. That seems like a lot. Yet white cells usually make up less than 1 percent of blood. Different types of white cells perform different jobs in the immune system. Along with certain chemicals in the plasma, they target and attack anything that does not belong in the body.

Unwelcome Intruders

The immune system will attack thorns, slivers, inhaled smoke, and pollen. It will attack cancer cells that break loose from tumors. More often, it attacks microbes—germs such as viruses and bacteria.

White blood cells, seen here attacking surgical thread, fight anything that does not belong in the body.

Not all microbes that live inside the human body are bad. Bacteria in the intestines, for example, make certain vitamins and break down undigested food. Microbes in other parts of the body produce chemicals that keep out disease-causing germs. The immune system will not destroy these helpers.

Yet it constantly seeks out those germs that cause illness.

Outer Protection

Most of the time, dangerous germs do not break through the body's outer defenses. Skin acts like a wall to keep out invaders. Germs cannot multiply on dry skin. On sweaty skin, chemicals in the sweat kill the germs.

In the nose, hairs and sticky mucus trap dust particles and germs. If any escape into the throat, tiny hairs sweep them upward. Then the dirt and germs can be coughed up or swallowed. If they are swallowed, stomach acid will destroy most of the microbes.

Other body fluids also guard against unwanted invaders. Saliva contains chemicals that kill many dangerous germs. The eyes tear up to destroy microbes on the eye surface.

The Body's Alarm System

These walls and traps do not always keep invaders out, though. For example, burns, slivers, or scrapes may hurt skin. These injuries must be repaired before harmful germs get into the blood and spread throughout the body. The immune system starts a process called **inflammation**.

Inflammation begins when damaged skin cells from a cut finger, for example, release chemicals.

These chemicals signal tiny blood vessels near the cut to widen. Now more blood can reach the injury. The skin around the cut becomes red and warm. This is a sign that the immune system is working.

Also, some of the liquid blood plasma leaks through openings in the stretched-out vessels. This extra fluid causes the damaged area to swell up

This boy's eye is inflamed. Inflammation allows extra blood cells to reach an injury and repair damaged skin cells.

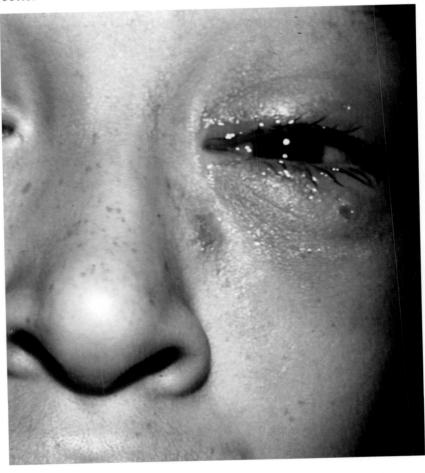

The Immune System Fights Disease

and press against nearby nerve cells. The injured person feels pain. Plasma also waters down poisons produced by germs. It also contains special healing ingredients.

Cells That Eat Germs

In addition to plasma, the immune system sends other fighters to the scene. Certain wandering white cells, called **phagocytes**, follow the chemical trail to the injury. The word *phagocyte* is a Greek term meaning eater cell. There are two kinds of eater cells. The smaller, more plentiful type reaches the injury quickly. They squeeze though the blood-vessel walls. They cling to germs and gobble them up. Then chemicals inside the phagocytes destroy the unwanted microbes. Within a few hours, the germ-filled white cells die. Now other cell eaters must clear these dead cells from the area.

Several hours later, larger phagocytes arrive at the scene. When they leave the blood vessels, these latecomer white cells get even bigger. They are then called **macrophages**—big eaters. Macrophages chew up germs, too. They also act as garbage collectors. First, they change shape. Like a mittened hand grabbing a pebble, they surround invading germs, germ-filled cells, or dead body cells. Then they eat them.

Usually this inflammation process works well. Macrophages live to continue their cleanup work

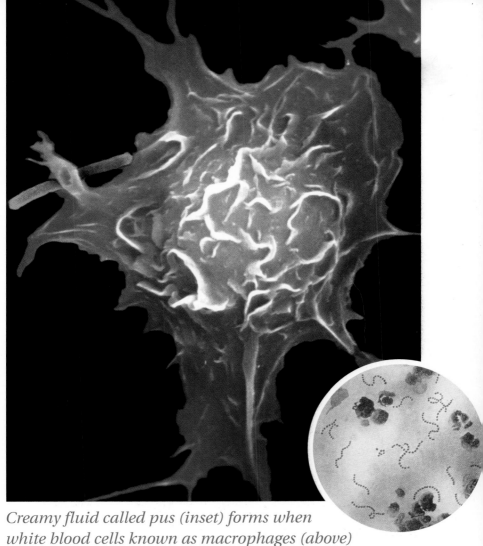

Creamy fluid called pus (inset) forms when white blood cells known as macrophages (above) destroy germs too slowly.

for weeks. During this time, new body cells repair the cut. Sometimes, though, macrophages do not work fast enough. Dead cells pile up and form a creamy substance called **pus**. This is a bad sign. Healing cannot begin until the pus is drained off.

Other problems occur when germs break through all body defenses. Certain types of germs get into body cells. They destroy them from the inside out. Other germs stay in the bloodstream. The poisons they produce kill cells.

Heating Up

The immune system works differently when germs spread inside the body. Macrophages send out a chemical signal. This signal tells the body to raise its temperature, causing a fever. The increased temperature makes the body hold back the iron and zinc needed by bacteria to copy themselves— reproduce. At the same time, fever causes phago- cytes to reproduce quickly. The phagocytes send a message for help to specialized white cells. Now all cells and chemicals of the immune system team up. They begin a full-scale battle against harmful invaders.

Chapter 2

Specialists at Work

Every day the bone marrow releases about 1 billion specialist white cells called **lymphocytes**. Scientists once thought all lymphocytes were the same. Now they know that each of these special white cells is an expert at targeting just one kind of germ. Maybe just one lymphocyte out of 5 million will recognize a bit of measles virus, for instance. When the virus, or a cell containing the virus, enters the body and bumps into that lymphocyte, it sets off a chain reaction. Specially shaped markers on the surface of the lymphocyte attach to a measles-virus marker. Like a key in a lock, the markers join and tighten. Once the markers fit securely, the lymphocyte produces many more measles specialists—copies of itself to attack the virus. Lymphocytes take three to seven days to make enough tight-fitting copies to be useful.

Lymphocytes have surface markers long before they meet any germs. Some lymphocytes have the markers before they leave the bone marrow. Others get them after they pass through a gland in the chest called the thymus.

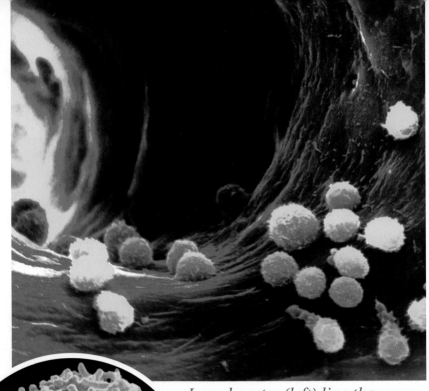

Lymphocytes (left) line the inside of an artery (above). Lymphocytes recognize and destroy germs in the blood.

Lymphocyte Storage Areas

Certain parts of the body are packed full of lymphocytes with many different surface markers. These areas are usually where lymphocytes first bump into their attackers. Some of these stored white cells will never be used. Still, they lie in wait for their matching germs to pass through.

Perhaps the most well-known lymphocyte ware-houses are in the throat. There, tonsils and adenoids help destroy germs that are breathed in or swallowed. If too many germs enter, tonsils and adenoids may not be able to handle the infection. They become diseased and have to be removed. That does not seem to affect the immune system, though. Scientists think other storage spots may share the extra work. For example, extra tonsil tissue in back of the tongue may take over. Also, lympho-cyte patches in the intestines can act on swallowed germs.

The largest lymphocyte warehouse is the spleen, an organ near the stomach. Lymphocytes recog-nize and destroy germs in blood that enter the spleen.

Other important storage places—**lymph nodes**—are scattered throughout the body. Less than one inch long, these bean-shaped nodes are found in the armpits, below the hips, and in the neck region. Nodes remove germs from plasma that has left the bloodstream. About three liters of this plasma leaks from the blood vessels into body tissues every day. After passing through the lymph nodes, the cleaned tissue fluid returns to the bloodstream through spe-cial vessels.

During a serious infection, the nodes swell up. That is because lymphocytes are multiplying quickly —another sign of the immune system at work. Germs and germ-filled macrophages bump into lymphocytes in the nodes. By chance, they may encounter their match. Then these specialized white cells go into action. They prepare to defend the body.

Helper Lymphocytes

Not all lymphocytes with markers for the same germ have the same job. The most important job is that of a helper. Without helpers, the other lymphocytes cannot do their work.

Helper lymphocytes do not directly destroy the germ. First a germ-filled macrophage must show them a piece of the invader. This is what happens: When a macrophage chews up a germ, it sends tiny bits of the microbe to its outer surface. Like a blind person feeling his way around, the macrophage travels through the lymph nodes. If the proper helper lymphocyte bumps into the macrophage, the helper attaches to the germ bit. The helper then shows that piece to other lymphocytes with different jobs. If they have markers for the germ, the helper instructs them to divide or copy themselves. Helper lymphocytes allow the immune-system chain reaction to continue.

Killer Lymphocytes

Certain lymphocytes are killers. They attach to the surface of body cells infected with germs. Then a signal from helpers lets them copy themselves.

Killers punch holes in the germ-filled body cells. Water and salts enter the cell and it bursts. The

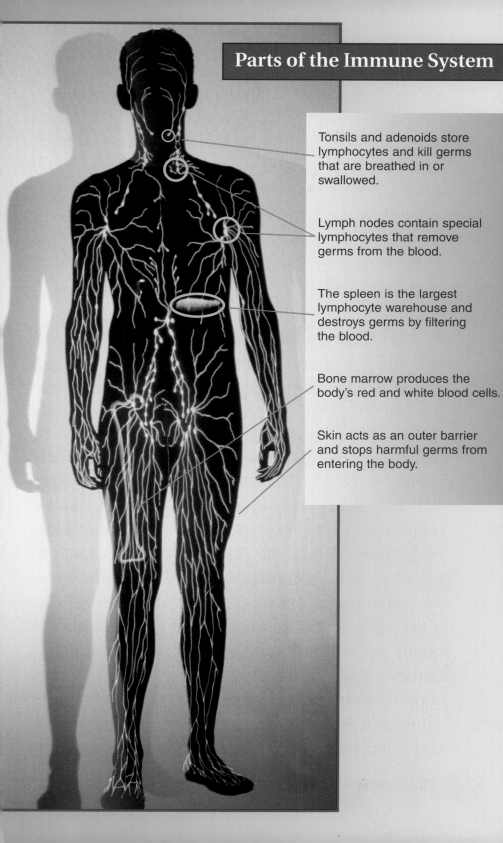

Parts of the Immune System

Tonsils and adenoids store lymphocytes and kill germs that are breathed in or swallowed.

Lymph nodes contain special lymphocytes that remove germs from the blood.

The spleen is the largest lymphocyte warehouse and destroys germs by filtering the blood.

Bone marrow produces the body's red and white blood cells.

Skin acts as an outer barrier and stops harmful germs from entering the body.

targeted cell dies, but so do the germs. Lab experiments show killers also target single cancer cells.

After attacking one cell, a killer goes on to attack others. It does this as long as it receives two signals. One comes from helper lymphocytes. The other comes from the cell under attack. Unless it gets both signals, the killer lymphocyte will destroy itself. Scientists are not sure why this happens. They believe the double signal acts as a safety measure so the wrong cells are not damaged.

Antibody Producers

Still other lymphocytes produce Y-shaped proteins called **antibodies**. These antibody-making lymphocytes cannot act on germs inside body cells. Instead, they must attach directly to part of an invading germ or poison made by a germ. Then, encouraged by helper cells, these lymphocytes start to divide themselves many times. Now the copied cells begin making up to 10 million antibodies an hour. They release them into body fluids such as blood. These antibodies will only lock onto germ parts that match areas on their particular Y shape.

Even then, antibodies do not directly destroy germs or poisons. They just mark them for destruction by the less specialized phagocytes. For example, certain antibodies attack poisons made by bacteria. They turn the poisons into solid clumps. Others cause germs to lump together. These clumps and

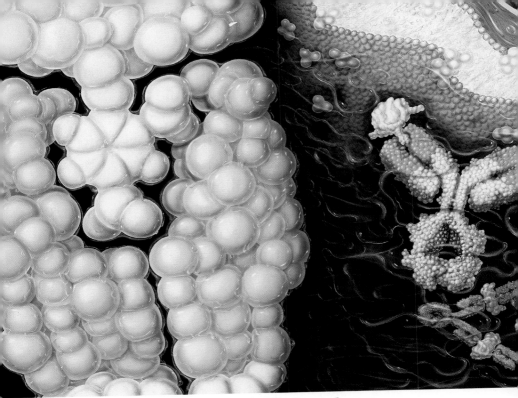

Y-shaped proteins called antibodies attack germs.

lumps are easy for phagocytes to find and gobble up. Still other antibodies coat germs with chemicals that lure phagocytes to the microbes.

Few antibodies remain after the germs have been destroyed. Yet if the same germs invade again, the cells that make those antibodies can be quickly reactivated.

Memory Cells

Usually when a person recovers from a germ-caused disease, he or she is safe from that particular illness for months, years, or sometimes a lifetime. He or she develops a natural immunity. This happens because some of the copies made by the original lymphocytes were not used up. All types of leftover lymphocytes can become memory cells. If that same disease germ enters the body a second time, its memory cells recognize it. They start copying themselves right away. Killer lymphocytes go into action. Antibody makers produce many more anti-bodies faster than in the first infection. Usually these forces can destroy the invaders before signs of illness appear.

Specialized white blood cells called lymphocytes attack a cancer cell (red, middle).

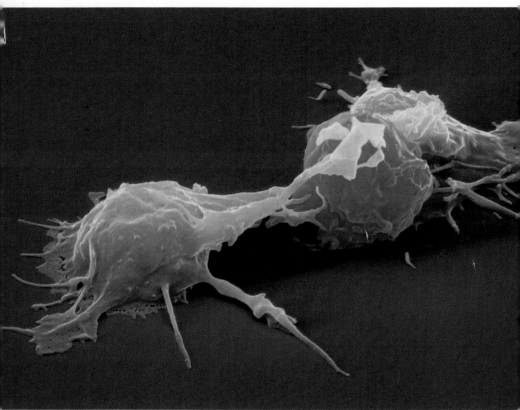

The Immune System

Scientists still have a lot to learn about how these immune cells work. For example, they once believed that only humans and other animals with backbones—**vertebrates**—made antibodies. Now scientists have found substances similar to vertebrate antibodies in cockroaches. By experimenting with these insects, they hope to better understand the human immune system. Then they can use this knowledge to help solve immune-system problems.

Chapter 3

Problems of the Immune System

Sometimes people are born with or develop an immune system that does not work properly. In certain cases, it does not work at all. Doctors are constantly searching for ways to correct these immune-system problems.

Allergies and Anaphylaxis

Some people have immune systems that overreact to common substances: animal dander, insect poisons, plant pollen, dust, cosmetics, even certain foods and some medicines. Immune cells see these substances, or **allergens**, as enemies and try to fight them off. The reactions allergens cause are called allergies.

First contact with an allergen usually produces no visible signs. Instead, it causes lymphocytes to produce large amounts of antibodies. These antibodies cover the surface of certain body cells in the area of contact. After a second contact, the allergen causes the antibody-coated cells to release strong

Allergens such as pollen (inset) and insect poison cause reactions in the immune system known as allergies.

chemicals. Now signs of allergy appear: runny noses, itchy eyes, skin rashes, vomiting. Certain allergens—aspirin, for example—may even cause reactions without antibody production.

Almost anything that causes allergies can trigger a more dangerous reaction—**anaphylaxis**. In super-allergic people, eating a peanut or being stung by a bee can make the immune system go wild. Cells release dangerous chemicals in all parts of the body, not just the contact area. Blood pressure drops suddenly. Breathing becomes difficult. Without fast treatment, the person could suffer serious damage or even die within minutes. People who know they have these dangerous reactions carry special medicine with them at all times. Whenever possible, they stay away from the substance causing their problem. They also carry cards or ID tags that inform hospital workers of their condition.

Immune-system overreactions can be harmful. Yet victims of another dangerous illness have immune systems that do not work at all.

Bubble Boy

Babies born with severe combined immunodeficiency disease, SCID for short, cannot fight off germs. Everything around SCID babies has to be germfree. Otherwise, they will die of simple infections. Here is the story of one SCID baby who helped doctors find the cause of this condition.

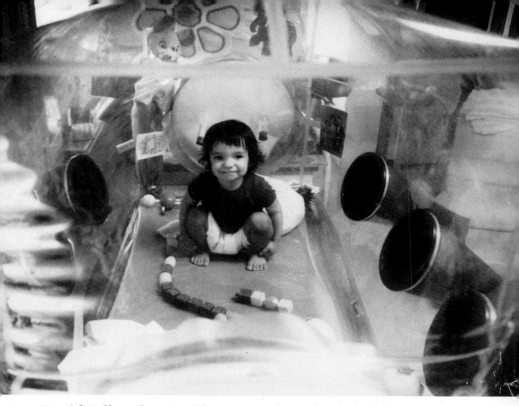

David Veller plays inside a germ-free plastic bubble. David was born with an immune system that could not fight off germs.

David Veller was born in Texas in 1972. His parents asked the doctors to do something to protect their son. Maybe, if David lived long enough, someone would find a cure. David's doctors and parents kept him in a germfree plastic bubble. Everything in the bubble had to be free of germs— the air, his toys, even his food. Special long gloves were built into the bubble. Nurses put their hands into the gloves from an opening on the outside. This was the only way they could feed and change David. As David got older, he used the gloves in the opposite direction to handle his homework.

David Veller wears a protective suit while playing outside.

David lived in this plastic home for twelve years. During that time, doctors tried to cure him. They put healthy bone marrow into David's body. They hoped the new cells would replace David's unhealthy ones. It did not work.

When David died in 1984, some of his cells were still growing in a laboratory dish. Scientists used these cells to discover an absence of a certain chemical that causes SCID to develop. Now, before families have children, doctors can test them for that chemical. Thanks to David, families can know their chances of having a SCID baby.

Even better, in 2002, doctors from Italy and Israel removed bone marrow in two SCID children. They made changes in the bone marrow cells so the cells could make the missing chemical. Then the doctors put the altered marrow cells back into the children. So far, these children appear to have healthy immune systems. Of course, it will be years before the doctors know how well the treatment worked.

Still, these children now can hope for a long and healthy life. Meanwhile, victims of another disease are waiting for new discoveries that will destroy a deadly virus.

AIDS

HIV is a virus that disables the immune system. It causes a disease called acquired immune deficiency syndrome, or AIDS. HIV mainly lives and reproduces in helper lymphocytes. Then the new viruses burst out and spread to other helpers. These diseased helpers cannot signal killer cells to reproduce and attack. In other words, HIV damages the very cells that should be fighting it.

The HIV virus reproduces inside a lymphocyte (inset) before bursting out and infecting other helper cells (below).

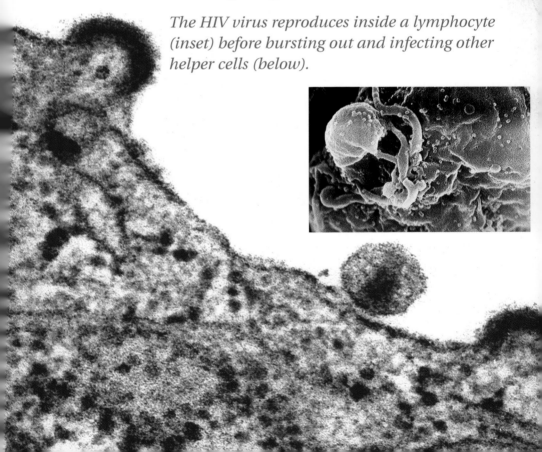

People infected with HIV may appear healthy for years. Yet gradually the number of their helper white cells goes down. They develop signs of AIDS such as fever and swollen lymph nodes. They tire easily and lose weight. Although antibodies to HIV do appear in the blood, they cannot get at viruses hidden away in the helper cells. Even so, testing for HIV antibodies is one way doctors know if a person has been infected with the virus.

With damaged immune systems, AIDS patients can easily fall victim to diseases such as tuberculosis, pneumonia, or cancer. Doctors can treat these diseases. Doctors also have treatments that will extend the life of an AIDS victim. Yet, so far, nothing completely gets rid of the virus. Scientists continue to look for a cure or a way to prevent AIDS. After much testing, they have discovered something in saliva that blocks the action of HIV. This could be an important step in their search.

While the AIDS virus destroys lymphocytes, in other diseases the immune system itself damages healthy body cells.

Autoimmune Diseases

In autoimmune diseases, killer lymphocytes and antibodies destroy their own body's cells. Rheumatoid arthritis is one example of an autoimmune disease. This illness affects young or middle-aged women three times as often as men. The immune cells attack joints. Knees, hips, wrists, neck, elbows, and ankles become swollen and painful—signs of inflammation. People with rheumatoid arthritis do have times when they feel better. Then, without warning, the pain begins again. Patients can help control their pain by resting, doing mild exercises, and taking aspirin or similar medicines. Sometimes, though, a joint becomes so badly damaged the person cannot move. Then doctors may replace it with one manufactured of metal and plastic.

Scientists continue to search for a cure for AIDS.

Multiple sclerosis, another autoimmune disease, affects people who are between fifteen and forty years old. The immune system damages a special coating on nerve cells. This causes short circuits in the signals sent through nerves to muscles. Gradually the person becomes weak and clumsy. Damaged eye muscles cause vision problems. Taking a chemical made by healthy immune cells helps some patients. In 2001, doctors tried a new treatment. They removed healthy nerve cells from

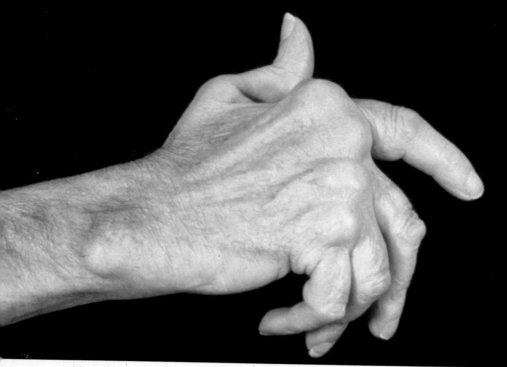

Rheumatoid arthritis affects a person's hand, causing painful swelling and damaged joints.

the ankle of a multiple sclerosis patient. They injected them into a damaged area in his brain. In time, doctors hope these cells will repair the nerve coating on the brain cells. This is just one of many experiments to cure autoimmune diseases. Meanwhile, scientists are trying to learn the causes of these illnesses. Then they may be able to keep them from happening. In fact, scientists already have found ways to prevent some diseases spread by germs.

The Immune System

Chapter 4

Man-Made Immunity

In cases where diseases are very dangerous, scientists have worked to create ways to control them. Diseases such as smallpox, for example, blinded, scarred, and even killed many people all over the world. In the mid-1950s, polio severely disabled many people. These illnesses have almost disappeared, thanks to injections of dead, old, or weakened microbes—**vaccines**.

Vaccines are not available for every germ-caused illness. Also, some vaccines, like those for flu, do not work as well as others. One reason is that the virus shape changes often. This tricks the immune system into not recognizing it. Also, there are many types of flu viruses. Only a few of them can be put into a single vaccine. Scientists must make educated guesses about what type of flu will occur each year. Yet flu vaccines protect 70 to 90 percent of healthy adults. Vaccines are still the best way to prevent germ-caused diseases.

Vaccine solutions may contain whole germs or pieces of germs. When injected into the body, these vaccines cause the immune system to produce antibodies just as live, strong microbes do. More importantly, they usually do this without causing illness. For some diseases, the vaccine's effect may lessen after a while. Then the body needs a booster shot every few years to pep up the immune system. Researchers spent many years learning these things.

Hundreds of years ago, doctors knew nothing about microbes or the immune system. Then, after the microscope was invented, European scientists were able to see tiny germs and cells. Over time, they learned how the body reacts to germs. These discoveries led to better ways to make vaccines for smallpox and other dangerous diseases. In the 1960s,

Health care workers inject a girl with polio vaccine.
Vaccines are an important part of controlling disease.

The Immune System

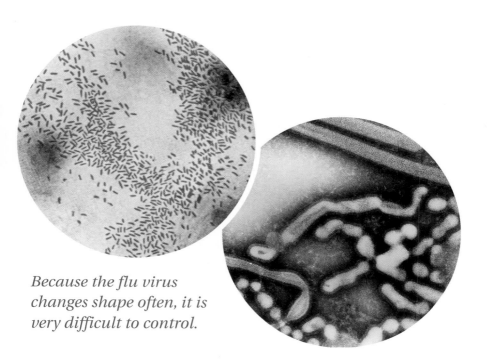

Because the flu virus changes shape often, it is very difficult to control.

doctors gave smallpox shots to children all over the world. As a result of this huge effort, the last known case of smallpox was reported in 1977. Doctors stopped giving the vaccine. Still, health care workers stay alert in case smallpox appears again. They also watch for outbreaks of other diseases.

Short-Term Treatments

When people who are not immune are exposed to a dangerous germ, they need instant antibodies. In such cases, doctors inject blood plasma with antibodies in it. They get this plasma from someone who already had the vaccine or who has recovered from the disease. These ready-made antibodies will not last as long as those the body makes. On the other hand, they work immediately. Doctors recently used this method when post office workers were exposed to anthrax bacteria. Men and women in the armed forces who had been given the anthrax vaccine donated their plasma to the postal workers.

While shots of human plasma are best, human volunteers often cannot provide enough plasma for any particular disease. Then scientists use plasma from vaccinated animals, such as horses, goats, or sheep. When the animals build up enough antibodies, scientists remove some of their blood. They

Researchers test the safety of vaccines on lab animals such as mice and rats.

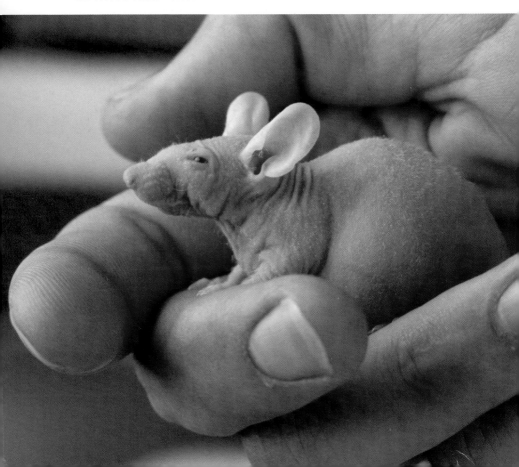

separate the plasma and store it in refrigerators until needed.

What Lies Ahead?

Animal and human cells contain chemical codes for making different types of antibodies. Scientists have been able to insert the human code into cow cells so the cows produce both human and cow antibodies in their milk. Researchers have yet to figure out a way to have the cow make only human antibodies.

Scientists are also experimenting with plant cells as antibody factories. The scientists grew plant antibodies, or "plantibodies," for a germ that causes a form of tooth decay. In 1998, they rubbed these plantibodies onto the teeth of human volunteers. The results were positive: They did prevent decay. Still, scientists need to do much more testing.

In addition to making plantibodies, scientists are using plants as containers for vaccines. They insert bits of germs into food-plant cells. New plants grown from the altered ones also have the germ bits in them. Eating these plants activates the immune system just as an injected vaccine does. The tough, outer walls of plant cells protect the vaccine from stomach acid. Scientists have grown vaccines in potatoes, bananas, melons, and tomatoes. European scientists have even used a vaccine in black-eyed peas to protect minks from a viral disease. In tests so far, the food vaccines act normally in animals and people.

Poor countries could benefit from these plant vaccines if the plants could be grown locally. This would cost much less than importing the injected variety. Also, they do not need to be refrigerated. Best of all, they taste good and are painless.

Cause for Concern

While these new discoveries show promise, some people are concerned. They object to placing codes from human or germ cells into plants and animals. They argue that this may create problems researchers have not yet considered. For example, will altered plants spread out from where they are grown? If so, will they breed with normal food plants and pass on the code? More important, what will happen to the immune systems of people who eat these plants? Scientists continue to look for answers to these questions.

Meanwhile, researchers are experimenting with other painless ways to give vaccines. They are working on a vaccine for AIDS that can be given in nose drops. So far, this has worked on tests with monkeys, but it has yet to be tried on humans. Also, a new spray for measles vaccine was used on more than two thousand children. Tests done in South Africa showed this prevented measles better than the injected vaccine. The doctor sprays the

Experimenting with vaccinated animals like this rat is important to understanding how the immune system fights disease.

inside of a paper mask with the vaccine and places the mask over the child's nose and mouth. The patient breathes it in for thirty seconds. Possibly these methods could be used for any disease caused by germs that enter through the nose and mouth.

No specific germ is known to cause cancer. Yet an experimental cancer treatment uses certain bacterial vaccines to kick-start the immune system. Still other

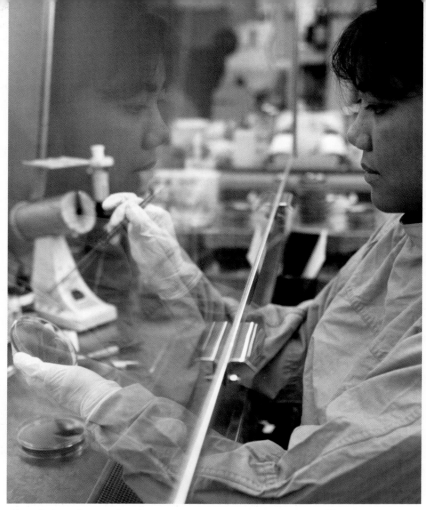

Studying how the immune system operates allows scientists to create better and safer ways to treat diseases.

cancer treatments use vaccines made from cancer cells or from the patient's own killer lymphocytes.

Every day scientists continue to uncover more secrets of the immune system. They exchange information with researchers all over the world. Their discoveries will lead to better and safer ways of treating and preventing diseases.

allergen: A common substance that causes some immune systems to overreact. Examples of reactions are rashes, runny noses, sneezing, and vomiting.

anaphylaxis: A severe reaction to an allergen that could cause death.

antibodies: Y-shaped proteins that coat or clump germs. Antibodies are made by certain white blood cells.

bone marrow: Central area in a bone where blood cells are formed.

inflammation: Redness, heat, and swelling in damaged body tissues.

lymph nodes: Storage areas for lymphocytes.

lymphocytes: Specialized white blood cells that are part of the immune system.

macrophages: Large phagocytes that patrol the body for several weeks eating germs and dead body cells.

oxygen: A gas needed by all living things.

phagocytes: Cells that eat germs and debris.

plasma: The liquid part of blood.

platelets: Bits of cells formed in the bone marrow that help blood to clot.

pus: Dead bacteria and cells that collect in an infected area.

vaccines: Man-made solutions of dead or weakened germs or bits of germs.

vertebrates: Animals with backbones.

Books

Frances R. Balkwill, *Cell Wars*. Minneapolis: Lerner, 1994. Describes the white blood cells and how they defend the body against viruses and bacteria. This book also discusses vaccination as a way to prevent certain illnesses. Illustrations are cartoon style.

Jackie Hardie, *Blood and Circulation*. Crystal Lake, IL: Rigby Interactive Library, 1997. Follows blood from the heart to its return. Explains the immune process, immune disorders, and how to stay healthy. Contains many photos and drawings.

Norbert Landa and Patrick A. Baeuerle, *Your Body's Heroes and Villains*. Hauppauge, NY: Forest House, Barron's Educational Series, 1997. Professor Gene's Micro Machine travels through the body to examine the cells and chemicals in the blood that fight disease germs. This book includes large, colorful drawings and diagrams.

Steve Parker, *Blood*. Brookfield, CT: Copper Beech Books, 1997. Explains how blood circulates, describes the cells it contains, and shows how white blood cells fight infection. It also discusses immune disorders. This book is illustrated with many diagrams and photographs.

Websites

American Society of Microbiology (www.microbe. org). This website answers questions about the safety of vaccination on its Microbes in the News— Down With Vaccines link.

Food and Drug Administration (www.healthfinder. gov). Brief, kid-friendly description of childhood vaccinations and why they are needed.

Staying Healthy (www.KidsHealth.org). Medical experts discuss allergies, asthma, hives, and why kids have them.

What the Heck Is a DNA Vaccine? (people.Ku.edu). Describes how vaccines are made. Has links to information on antibodies.

Index

Picture Credits

Cover: © Russell Kightley/Photo Researchers, Inc.
© Bettmann/CORBIS, 7, 27
© BSIP/Photo Researchers, Inc., 21
CDC, 13 (inset), 29 (inset), 31, 34, 35 (both)
© CNRI/Photo Researchers, Inc., 16,
© Electron Microscopy Unit/Max Planck Institut, 25 (inset)
© Eye of Science/Photo Researchers, Inc., 22
© Oliver Meckes/Nicole Ottawa/Eye of Science/Photo Researchers, Inc., 8
© Dr. K.G. Murti/Visuals Unlimited, 13
PhotoDisc, 19, 25, 39, 40
© Keith R. Porter/Photo Researchers, Inc., 8
© Science VU/Visuals Unlimited, 28
© SIU/Visuals Unlimited, 32
© Uta Von Schwedler/University of Utah, 29
© Ted Spiegel/CORBIS, 36
© SPL/Photo Researchers, Inc., 16 (inset)
Dr. Weyand/CDC, 11

A former medical technologist and science teacher, Gloria Boudreau has written numerous fiction and nonfiction articles for children's magazines. Two of her stories won awards from the Society of Children's Book Writers and Illustrators. Ms. Boudreau lives with her husband, Robert, in South Hadley, Massachusetts.